Product
Planning Guide

Strategically design an integrated suite of products to leverage your experience and expertise

KURT BLACK

Dedication:

This planning guide is dedicated to all the hard working entrepreneurs out there that haven't yet built leverage into their businesses by productizing their experience and experience.

It's also dedicated to those that have already started this journey and realize they want to make their business even better. Continual improvement is the path to epic success.

Table of Contents

Part 1:
Introduction

First off, I want to thank you for picking up a copy of this planning guide. It complements our training and podcast over at leverageupproductmastery.com.

It's essentially a workbook . . . a workbook to guide you through the planning exercises. I was told not to call it a workbook because "people don't want to work" and they won't buy it. I hope that's not true of you. Of the numerous entrepreneurs, consultants, coaches and business executives I've had the great fortune to work with, I can't think of many that didn't want to work. In fact, most of them were hyper-workers. But in some cases, they just needed some guidance, some direction, some help with the strategic planning of their efforts.

These exercises will be extremely valuable if you're just getting started. They will also hopefully help you find some new insights if you've been at this awhile.

Because this is a "work book" meant to compliment other training, we will only be covering the various topics at a high level. More in-depth discussion of the framework and all of these topics are available in various resources on the website, and are discussed thoroughly on the podcast.

Chapter 1: The Product Suite Framework

Before we get started planning, it's important to make sure we're all clear on the product framework when it comes to a leveraged business. There are essentially two categories of products you will need: "front-end" and "back-end" products. These have do with your sales process, or what is sometimes called a sales funnel or a marketing funnel.

With a sales funnel, customers enter into the top or the "front-end" and then go through some sort of nurturing process that hopefully "converts" them into paying customers. The products that they buy are the "back-end" of the funnel. Diagram 1–1 illustrates this concept.

I like to think of front-end products as your marketing-oriented products. They are what attract your prospects. Using a fishing analogy, they are the 'bait." Back-end products are your revenue-generators.

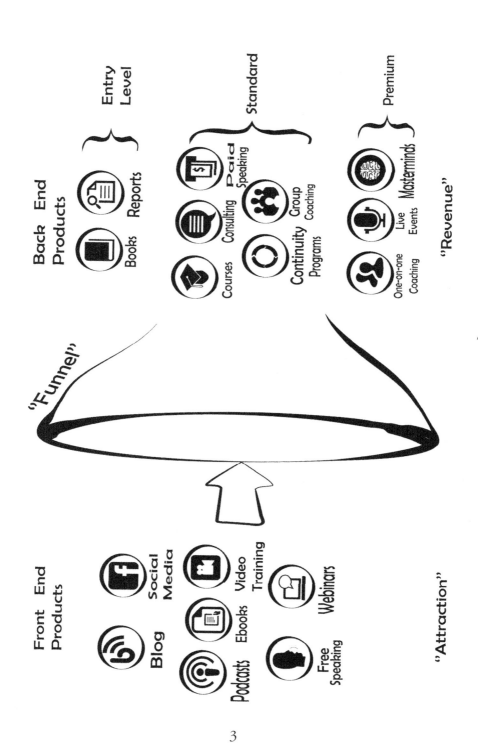

Back End Products

Entry Level

Reports

Books

Standard

Paid Speaking

Consulting

Courses

Group Coaching

Continuity Programs

Premium

Masterminds

Live Events

One-on-one Coaching

"Revenue"

"Funnel"

Front End Products

Social Media

Blog

Video Training

Ebooks

Webinars

Podcasts

Free Speaking

"Attraction"

3

Chapter 2:
Some Key Planning
Concepts

In addition to the overall product framework, it's important to understand a few additional key concepts. These will be important as we get into the planning process.

Alignment

The first key concept is called alignment. It has to do with the overall "alignment" of your products from the "front" to the "back" of your funnel. This is critical, because the more aligned your product suite is, the more successful you're going to be. Let's go back to the fishing analogy. Let's say your overall goal is to catch a fish (make a sale). If our goal is to catch a fish, but we're using the wrong bait (front-end products), we're not going to be very successful.

Everything from the front to the back of the sales process needs to be aligned so that we're attracting and capturing the right prospects that will ultimately want and be a good fit for our back-end products.

Without alignment, we can end up spending a lot of time and money attracting the "wrong" type of prospects—the ones that will never buy our products, or worse yet, the ones that buy them but aren't a fit for our product / business.

Have you ever been on a fishing trip and brought the wrong type of bait? Alignment is critical.

Splintering

"Splintering" is a term I first heard from Ryan Deiss and his team at Digital Marketer. I don't know if he first coined it, but it's where I heard it first. Splintering has to do with using pieces of your "core" product to attract potential buyers. You are slicing off, or splintering, pieces of your core product to provide as teasers or introductions to your full product. You are taking a piece of your core product and using it to attract prospects.

In essence, this is what a restaurant does when it hands out free samples. They're offering you a "taste" of the core product they're trying to sell in order to get you interested. If you were trying to sell amazing tasting cakes, you wouldn't try to attract people with a sample of your BBQ sandwich, would you?

This is the concept of splintering, and it will be critically important as you design your front-end products to attract prospects into your sales funnel.

Part II: Begin with the End in Mind

When designing their products, a lot of people want to start at the beginning of the whole process—building a following. They say to themselves, "Well I don't need to worry about a product yet because I don't have a list." Or they think," I need to build my list so I need to come up with something to attract them."

When it comes to proactively designing your business, these ways of thinking are a mistake. You want to design a business that (A) ends up being something YOU love doing on a day-to-day basis (hey, if you have the opportunity to design the business you'll be doing day-after-day for the next number of years, you might as well build something you love, right?); and (B) it needs to be designed so that it's attracting your IDEAL customer. And you can't really design front-end products to attract these ideal customers if you don't know the final destination.

It's sort of like trying to go somewhere without a map and without any real information on your destination. What are your chances of getting there? You may end up there by luck, but you won't be very efficient about it. And your path there might be a long, winding, jumbled mess (and this is NOT what you want to build as

6

your customer experience—a long, winding jumbled mess of a journey to your revenue generating product). You want this to be a nice, logical, efficient path that makes sense to your customers. That's why we need to start with the end in mind.

So let's begin at the ending, shall we?

Chapter 3: Common Backend Products

The first thing you're really going to want to think about is your back-end products. These are your revenue generating products and are the engine of your business.

If you're just getting started at this, you need to think about what types of products you would most enjoy marketing and delivering. Would you like to be speaking in front of audiences with your message? If so, maybe you need to focus on live events and paid speaking opportunities. Do you hate public speaking? Well, then you might want to focus on building online courses. Do you enjoy working with small groups of people? If so, you should consider group coaching and masterminding.

A bit of planning at the beginning of your journey will help ensure you end up with a business that you really love. I know plenty of entrepreneurs (myself included) that have built very successful businesses in terms of financial success, but that they have hated on a day-to-day business. You do NOT want to end up there. Or if you're already there, you want to effectively plan so that you can get out of there as fast as humanly possible.

If you're not just getting started at this, but rather have been at it for awhile, then these planning exercises are important in order or ensure that (1) all of your existing front-end and back-end products are in alignment to ensure the maximum success possible; and (2) you can smartly plan out your next back-end products or some additional front-end products, to more effectively convert prospects into paying customers.

So in order to help you with this planning, and to help you begin with the end in mind, let's first take a look at some of the most common back-end products and their respective pro's and con's.

Online Courses

Online courses are an excellent backend product for teaching a lot of content.

Pro's:
- Scalability—online courses are really great in terms of scalability, in terms of getting leverage. They can be offered online, so you can reach such a wide audience relatively easily
- Low Cost—They have relatively little fixed cost associated with them (relative to say a live event), so there is lower risk
- Profit Potential—again, because of the low cost structure, online courses have a huge advantage in terms of the potential for profit (this obviously depends on your specific market and what you can charge)

- Multi-Media (multi-modalities)—People learn in different ways. Some like watching video, some like listening to audio and some like reading. Online courses allow you to bring all these different modalities together into a single product. You can have videos that they watch, with a MP3 download for listening on the go, as well as downloads of the slides and other complimentary resources like worksheets, templates, checklists, etc.

- Great compliment to other products—Brendon Burchard advises to never sell tickets to an event . . . sell an online course and include (or discount) tickets to your event along with the course. This offers two key sales benefits: (1) people can get the training immediately and (2) it gives you a longer period of time to fill the event

Con's:

- Variety of Skills Required—In general, online courses require a variety of skills such as writing, video and an assortment of technical skills. This can sometimes be intimidating

- Time Requirement—Putting together a good course takes time. You need to plan it out, develop the scripts and/or slides, shoot videos, put together handouts among other things. It does take some time

Continuity Programs/Membership Sites

Continuity programs are where customers pay you on an ongoing, regular basis. Think monthly subscriptions. People join your membership site or continuity program and pay you $47 per month for example.

Pro's:

- Scalability—when done correctly, continuity programs are highly scalable. I say "done correctly" because you need to find items to offer that are scalable themselves. For example, if I were a consultant and offered everyone 5 hours of consulting, that's not very scalable because I need to provide 5 hours for each member each month. However, if I offer a group Q&A call every week or every month, that then is scalable because I can support multiple people at once

- Low Cost—Similar to online courses, they typically have relatively little fixed cost associated with them, particularly if your continuity program is offered online and you provide group coaching / support, training and other content via a "remote" model (webinar, videoconference, teleconference, etc.).

Con's:

- Variety of Skills Required—Similar to online courses, continuity programs require a variety of skills such as writing, video and an assortment of technical skills. This can sometimes be intimidating

- The biggest drawback of continuity programs, particularly membership sites, is that it can be REALLY hard to get them going. This is particularly true if part of your value is interaction amongst the members (e.g., a private Facebook group). You need to reach critical mass in order for the value, interaction, etc to start to kick in, and then you need to maintain it.
- Another big drawback of the continuity program product is that people are constantly cycling in and out. Statistics show that paying customers of a monthly continuity program typically last 4-5 months on average. You therefore need to design special features into your program specifically designed at keeping them from dropping out.

Books

I often have clients tell me that they want to write a book to generate some cash to allow them to build all these other products they have in mind. Myth busting alert: books make really POOR back-end (revenue generating) products in general. Very few authors, especially first-time authors, make any money selling books.

They can however make great front-end products, which we'll cover later in this planning guide.

Here are the pro's and con's of book specifically as a back-end product:

Pro's:

- They don't require a large variety of skills, particularly technical skills
- Books still hold a lot of value in terms of perception of the author as an expert (people still really view authors of books in a higher light)

Con's:

- It's extremely hard to make any real money (directly) by selling books. In order to reach a decent sales volume, you typically need either a publisher or a large list / network. If you're just getting started, you probably don't have the latter yet. And a published is going to want a decent percentage of the profits
- Getting a publisher for a first time author can be extremely challenging and/or expensive ("pay to play" publishing model)

Paid Speaking Events

Paid speaking gigs are specifically those where you are paid an appearance fee. There are other types of speaking opportunities such as promotional speaking and selling-from-stage speaking.

Pro's:

- You are guaranteed revenue (per the terms of your contract)

- You can reach a large audience with your message and your expertise
- There are many places that pay speakers for a wide variety of topics (e.g., conferences)
- In general, it's not extremely difficult to get started. Yes, your speaking fees will go up as you get more experience, but in general it something that a beginning speaker can break into. Tip#1: get a booking agent if you're new (one that works on a commission basis). Tip #2: Start small to build a "portfolio" and references as fast as possible

Con's:

- You will need to speak in public. Aaaacckk! (#1 fear of Americans). If you don't like public speaking, you will have some work to do on this one
- You might need to live with lower-end speaking fees for a little while until you build up a portfolio and a list of testimonials
- Get your suitcase ready . . . there's some travel associated with this one (you may think list this as a "pro" but trust me, this moves to the 'con' list eventually for many)

Live Events/Training

I personally LOVE live events. I love the energy. I love the networking. I usually come back from an event pumped up. I also love delivering training—large groups, small groups, whatever.

Live events would include workshops, retreats, conferences and so forth.

Pro's:

- You can really make an impact at live events
- High energy, high level of interaction with your customers
- Can charge premium prices for live events

Con's:

- Live events can be expensive to produce, therefore you don't typically see the same profit margins in live events as with other products
- They are a risk. Yes, people can lose money putting on an event. You need to know what you're doing or hire someone that does. You often need to be "on the hook" for certain expenses (e.g., guaranteed room nights). Advice: start small.
- They can take a lot of time and energy to plan and produce. Most of the top event leaders are drained at the end of their multi-day events
- You generally need to spend a lot more time promoting a live event vs. an online course. It takes time and effort to get the commitments from people to attend live events these days

Group Coaching/Masterminds

If you haven't been part of a mastermind group, they are groups of individuals getting together to discuss a common topic. For example, there are many masterminds where business owners get together to discuss issues and help one another with their businesses. Sometimes these mastermind groups are focused on specific topics such as online marketing, or customer service as examples.

Pro's:

- Running mastermind groups is great because you get to work with some incredible individuals.
- You also get to leverage the knowledge and experience of the various individuals to make significant (and often rapid) impacts in the group members' businesses
- You can often charge a premium for this product (often a high end offering)

Con's:

- Masterminds and group coaching can sometimes be tricky to get started. It can sometimes be a catch 22. You need "prominent" members to attract other members, but the "prominent" members are going to want other prominent members in the group to mastermind with. I call these your "anchor" members. You need to get a critical mass in order to start getting some momentum rolling.

Notes:

17

Notes:

Chapter 4:
Designing My Ideal
Business

Okay, so it's time to get down to it now. Time to start planning. Write down some products that interest you in terms of generating revenue. There are some blank pages here for you to brainstorm some ideas.

Key Questions to Consider:

- What End-Products would I enjoy creating, marketing and delivering for the next several years?
- What end-products am I good at?
- How does my market most like to learn?
- Is there a product I could offer in my market that would make me unique? Stand out?

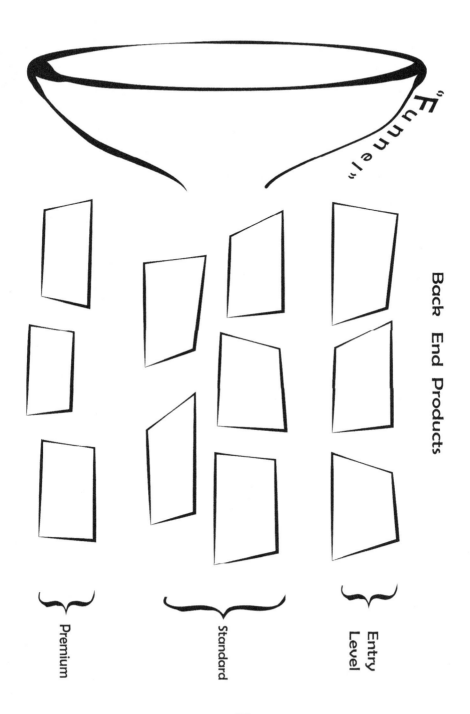

"Funnel"

Back End Products

Premium

Standard

Entry
Level

Notes:

Notes:

Notes:

Notes:

Part III:
Front-End Alignment

As we discussed earlier, alignment is critical. Our front-end products need to align with our core, revenue-generating products in order to maximize our success.

This section will help us plan the front-end of our sales process so that it perfectly aligns with the back-end.

Chapter 5: Common Front-End Products

Back-end products are about the revenue. Front-end products are all about the marketing. The goal of these front-end products is to attract prospects to our business and to convert them into customers.

To this end, there is an interesting and not always obvious paradox to our product structure: our best stuff needs to be on the front end. We need to give away our best stuff, our best ideas up front. This is what will attract customers. This can sometimes not feel right, but trust me, it's true.

By offering our best tips, our best advice, our best training up front, we will attract the most customers to our paid products. People's reaction is to think . . . wow, if his/her free stuff is this good, I can't wait to get the full product.

Below are some common products offered on the front-end of an effective sales funnels and a discussion of their pro's and cons.

Blog/Website

Blogs are probably one of the more common front-end products. Blogs are essentially a series of online articles commonly organized by topic/category.

Pro's:

- Very easy to create and keep updated
- Can generate a lot of exposure if you can build a following and increase interaction /sharing of your content

Con's:

- There aren't really a lot of cons
- Many people find the process of writing a lot of content to be burdensome

Webinars

Webinar are online versions of live presentation and seminars.

Pro's:

- Can reach a large number of potential prospects
- The fixed costs of conducting a webinar are significantly lower than those of a live event
- When marketed correctly, you can get a larger number of people to attend a webinar rather than a live event

Con's:

- Webinars take some level of technical ability
- Webinars can (although not often) have technical glitches during the event itself

- It is challenging to get people that register to actually show up ("things come up")
- It is challenging to keep the attention of those that attend the webinar (multi-tasking)
- Because they are online and not in person, they can be more challenging to close sales compared to when you're speaking to prospects live

Podcasts

Podcasts are big. These audio-based shows are easy to access with one's smartphone, so they allow your prospects to consume your content at a time that is convenient for them.

Pro's:
- You can access a large number of people
- There are some great platforms out there that make it easier for you to market your show and grow your audience (e.g., iTunes, Soundcloud)

Con's:
- For MOST people, there is a ton of technical equipment and processing that will be a challenge
- It takes a fair amount of time on an ongoing basis to book guests, conduct the interviews and produce the shows

- Depending on how professional you want the podcast to be, there could be a sizable investment in audio equipment required

Free Speaking Events

In contract to paid speaking events, these are unpaid (at least up front in the form of a speaking fee).

Pro's:
- Can reach a lot of people with your message
- Live speaking events are great lead generators
- If you're speaking for free, it is often expected (allowed) that you will be offering your products for sale (versus Paid Speaking gigs where you are often prohibited from selling your products from stage)

Con's:
- You often have to cover your travel (if any) and aren't guaranteed any revenue
- "Selling from stage" is a specialized skill and the pitch requires some planning and practice

Books

In contract to books as "back-end" products, books make excellent "front end" products.

Pro's:
- Books are great for adding to your credibility
- Books have become relatively easy to self-publish

Con's:
- Books can take a fair amount of time and effort to write (most people struggle with writing)

Notes:

Notes:

Chapter 6: Designing My Ideal Attraction (Marketing) Activities

As owners, founders and leaders of our businesses, a lot of the work we should be focused on is related to messaging, marketing and sales. These are typically the highest value activities of the founder entrepreneur. Since much of our time will be focused on these marketing-related activities, we want to make sure we enjoy the time as much as possible.

Key Questions:
- What types of front-end products would I enjoy working on for the next several years? Do I like to blog? Would I enjoy interviewing people via a regular podcast?
- What are my favorite modalities? (writing, speaking, talking/interviewing, etc.)
- What am I currently good at? (writing, speaking, talking/interviewing)?
- What modalities do my target audience enjoy most?
- What are the "super stars" in my industry doing?

Front End Products

"Funnel"

Notes:

Notes:

Notes:

Notes:

Part IV: Planning My Core Product

After putting some thought into our business at the 30,000 foot level, it's time to drill down into a little more detail. It's time to think about specifically what would our core offer be? As we discussed earlier, this is important to our planning efforts because we ideally want to "splinter" off sections of this core offer product to use on the front-end of our funnel to attract our ideal prospects.

Chapter 7:
Core Product Concept

At this time, I want you to really put some thought into your core offer product. If you already have your core offer product, then you can skim through this section and move on to the next exercise.

Some Key Questions To Consider:
- What is your overall topic?
- What are some titles for the product?
- What are the key Modules (Teaching Areas)? What would be a general outline?

Notes:

Notes:

Notes:

Notes:

Chapter 8:
Break It On Down

Now that you've put some definition around your core product offering, it's time to break it down further in order to identify some potential front-end products we could use to attract our ideal prospects.

Some Key Questions To Consider:
- What are some key tools or resources my audience would need in order to accomplish the objectives set forth in my core product?
- What pieces of my product could be used to "splinter" off a smaller product I could give away for free?
- Are there worksheets or templates I could give away?
- Are there case studies I could put together?
- Could I develop a cheat sheet or checklist that summarizes one specific component / chapter of my core product?

Trip Wire (Low-Priced Product)

The term "trip wire" comes from Ryan Deiss and his team at Digital Marketer as best I can tell. A trip wire is a very low-priced, entry level product (typically in the $1–$20 range). The key on pricing is to keep it in the "no brainer" range. Note that in certain markets where you core offer is extremely high priced (e.g., custom kitchen design), then your "trip wire price" may be priced higher. When you're talking about a $30,000 kitchen redesign, a $300 custom plan could be a trip wire.

The value and importance of the trip wire is that it converts prospects into customers... real, paying customers. There is something magical about people taking out their wallet and buying something from you, even something small. It is a huge psychological step in the prospect's mind, and it changes the relationship between the two of you. There also really is something to the notion that is puts people into a "buying mode."

It is critical that your trip wire product(s) be splintered off from your core offer product. It could be one chapter, one exercise, one something. But it makes the process of selling the bigger, core product much easier later on (you're essentially saying, "hey, if you liked that, you're really going to love this . . .")

Key Points When Designing Your Trip Wire Products:

- Best when splintered off the core product
- Should be in price range of $1–$20 (except in markets where core product is extremely high priced)

Notes:

Notes:

Notes:

Notes:

Lead Magnet

Lead Magnets are the "bait" in our overall sales and marketing efforts. They are the "products" we use to attract new prospects and to reward them for giving us their email address (opting-in to our list). In contrast to tripwire products, lead magnets are free (in monetary terms).

Just as the Tripwire product was splintered off your core product, you want to keep splintering down to get to effective lead magnets. Note that it may take you a bit of experimentation and testing to find really effective lead magnets. But in general, the best lead magnets are very specific, very targeted and solve a very specific problem for your prospects very quickly. You should try and design lead magnets that can be consumed and implemented by your prospects very quickly. Checklists, resource guides, case studies, and niche tools (e.g., a deal calculator) make great lead magnet products.

Key Points When Designing Your Lead Magnets
- Very specific solutions to very specific issues seem to work the best (remember you may have multiple lead magnets, so you're not trying to solve all their problems in one shot)
- The best lead magnets can be consumed and implemented quickly (this is why multi-day courses typically make poor lead magnets)
- Think in terms of tools, guides, checklists, diagrams, case studies and so forth
- Experimentation and testing will be key

Notes:

Notes:

Notes:

Chapter 9:
Man (or Woman) of Action

Okay, so you've done a lot of planning... now it's time to implement. Now you need to take action to bring the plan to life. Here are a few parting comments regarding execution of your product plan:

- The product creation process can get overwhelming at times. Stay the course. It will be worth it in the end. You will be amazed at the power of having your knowledge, experience and expertise productized

- Perfectionism is the enemy of progress/results. Many people (myself included) can get caught in the trap of wanting things to be perfect before we release them. They never will be. Get over it. Do your best. Release it. Get feedback. Improve. Do this over and over and you will achieve incredible success with your products.

- Always be thinking "alignment" across your front-end and back-end products

- Always be thinking "splintering" when developing your front-end products

- Stay focused on the 20%. People are busy. Most times, they want the "Cliff Notes" version of things. Keep this in mind as you're developing your products. It will help you develop products faster. It will help your customers get results faster.

Good luck to you! I'm looking forward to hearing about your success.

Part V:
Wrapping Things Up

You made it to the end of the exercises! Congratulations!! Now, remember that this product creation process is a journey. You will always be "iterating" to make your products better, to make them more impactful. Do not let perfectionism keep you from releasing your products.

Get Free Templates & Examples at:
www.LeverageupProductMastery.com/templates

Subscribe to the Podcast at:
www.LeverageupProductMastery.com/subscribe

About the Author

Kurt Black is a speaker, author, seminar leader and entrepreneur. He is the founder LeverageupProductMastery.com, an online community of entrepreneurs and business owners focused on packaging their knowledge, experience and expertise into salable products. This process of productization, allows us to build leverage in our businesses and in our lives.

He also is the host of the Product Mastery Podcast and the founder of LeverageUP Academy.